INTER ARMA

D1566569

COVER IMAGE
Jacob Aue Sobol

Cover and book design by Rebecca Wolff

Published in the United States by Fence Books, Science Library, 320
University at Albany, 1400 Washington Avenue, Albany, NY 12222

WWW.FENCEPORTAL.ORG

Fence Books are printed in Canada by The Prolific Group and
distributed by Small Press Distribution and Consortium Book Sales
and Distribution.

Library of Congress Cataloguing in Publication Data
Shufran, Lauren [1981-]
Inter Arma/Lauren Shufran

Library of Congress Control Number: 2013932325

ISBN I 3: 978-1-934200-68-1

FIRST EDITION
10 9 8 7 6 5 4 3 2

Fence Books are published in partnership with the University at
Albany and the New York State Writers Institute, and with help
from the New York State Council on the Arts and the National
Endowment for the Arts.

Earlier versions of some of these poems have appeared in *Aufgabe,
Perihelion,* and *Try!* Trafficker Press published a portion of the
text—also under the title *Inter Arma*—as a chapbook in 2011. Much
gratefulness, and much love, to all the editors.

Huge thanks, too, to Taylor Brady, Brandon Brown, Brent Cunning-
ham, Rachel Levitsky, and Erin Morrill, for questions, conversation,
and assistance with the difficult slash-and-burn.

And thank you, in all the places you are, Stacy Doris.

INTER ARMA

LAUREN SHUFRAN

FENCE
BOOKS

ALBANY, NEW YORK

OTTOLINE PRIZE

For Stacy, still keeping beat.

"For as for their wars," I said, "the manner in which they will conduct them is too obvious for discussion." "How so," said he. "It is obvious that they will march out together ...in order that, like the children of other craftsmen, they may observe the processes of which they must be masters in their maturity...for example the sons of potters look on as helpers a long time before they put their hands to the clay."
Plato
The Republic

The urn of language is so fragile.
Jacques Derrida
Cinders

Constructions of modern Western homosexuality in the United States do not distinguish between the penetrator and the penetrated . . . you are one, whichever position you assume. So if we revivify the dead metaphor "fag" on the bomb (an American catachresis for coward), then we are left with the notion that the U.S. military understands itself to be engaged in (albeit homicidal) homosexuality ...[this is] a frightening statement about how military masculinity conceives of sexuality as lethal penetration.
Carla Freccero
"They are all sodomites!"

On the branches of laurel
Saw two naked pigeons.
The one was the other
And the both of them no one.
Jack Spicer
"Ballad of the Shadowy Pigeons"

INTER ARMA

My epic was under construction—wars and armed violence
in the grand manner, with metre matching theme.

I had written the second hexameter when Cupid grinned
and calmly removed one of its feet.

Ovid, Amores

Afterwards They Photographed my Veteran Face, f/2 at 500,

The aperture where pussyfooting messes with
       My depth of field and fortitude—like o-
Ver-exposed lovers. Skeptical about my own
       Fidelity to form, I forged a hon-
Ey of the symptoms held indigenous to prop-
       Er honeys: prominence in cock and crock-
Ery. I douse this dish with glaze; it comes up lach-
       Rymose and glassy-mouthed, with fractures on
The arms of both my honey and his vassals. I
       Put the clay up on the wheel; I make a
Hole there. I was casting for our porcelain war when
       Cupid hacked into my gallery, en-
Feebling the pedestals exulting all my earth-
       Enware by glossing badly on my bisque and
Polishing the surfaces of haters. Plus our drill in-
       Structor's footsore 'cause his foot's up on the
Kiln where he's been kindling the grilling cells with
       Cinders of our difference. It's pretty tricky
Marching when your feet are fused to ovens. It's tough
       To wax prosodic when your metric's del-
Iquescing. I douse this dish with glaze 'cause it an-
       Neals and steels its scansion—not to mention
Waterlogging fixes mouths of jars that *make* my
       Fill of honeys. I throw the clay up on
The wheel; I get the air out with some wedging. I
       Think the Greeks persisted 'cause they threw down
Persian men with equal zeal, on Grecian vases.

My casting clay makes fractures in the shafts of Cupid's
      Arrows—plus it bottlenecks the fauces
Of our flasks for better throating. But I was think-
      Ing about sintering the powders of
Opponents when he came with porcelain face on like
      A pestle at my dynasty of dish-
Es. So countrymen, you know my gimp, and *get* dis-
      Memberment's what pitches longing onto
Cocks and itching pitchers. I throw these limbs into
      The kiln; they make a mold there. When they is-
Sue from the heat I glaze my vases like the Greeks
      Did, with these portraits of myself with mas-
Sive calves upon my camel as I'm bouncing out
      To war and swapping teacups at sympos-
Ia for potters. Suspicious of our zeal for missing
      Persons—and for *form*—I had invested
In this wheel to forge some hollows in these bodies
      Made of clay accrued from battlefields. I've
Got these master foot maneuvers on the pedals
      Of that wheel; I've got a master's thesis
On emoting on the skins of vassals. I throw my-
      Self up on the clay; it gets the air out,
Makes an absence. I'm all like, "*Okay*, Cupid." Aft-
      Erwards they photographed my barefoot face
At f-stops so *your* depth of pots is shallow. I
      Take the wheel; I turn it back. I throw my
Clay upon the earth. It makes a cut like kinship does.

Hazing Song

This account's the fiscal history of its *own*
        Discourse first, since I got versed in numis-
Matics, in which coins and birds and camel skins are
        All "small change" but if you lift them long e-
Nough you muscle out the balance. Plus luckily
        There's beaten tracks from currency, to
Words, to arms, to warfare. I mean I didn't *hit*
        That track—but probably I exercised
This stick while I was marching. This account's the fis-
        Cal tact you take with whom you have a brush
With in the outskirts. I suspected there was some-
        Thing cryptic up in that djellaba. I
Was sick for hearing speeches. I was fit to be
        All, "Go little book; into the mouths of
Strangers I deposit you; go earn some interest
        In their throats and make a little catalexis
Of their tellings." But probing men in robes is just
        Like poking sticks at writing, with that sob-
Er prickle in the repetition of its fic-
        Tion . . . plus that WikiLeak just published clips
Of coins all clinking in my purse and photographs
        Of me with all my slacks around my cank-
Les. It's a little like a pickle when you view
        It at that angle. It's like Aesop kis-
Sing earthenware while Delphians are clashing o-
        Ver sacrificial chickens. Which's why to
Make this book, I only *said* it: it's tough to pin
        A nomad down and tell him he's misspok-
En. It's tough to tell a horsefly not to keep his
        Buzzing localized—particularly
When you tell it from a village crammed with horses.

4

But Aesop wasn't thinking ostracism, fond-
      Ling that goblet; he was coveting
The calves of Greeks relaxing on its finish. And
      It wasn't fables Socrates was fish-
Ing for in suburbs, but the apotropes that he
      Could grope when skipping past its limits . . . plus
That manuscript that Phaedrus shielded up in his
      Djellaba. It makes you want to take a
Stick and exercise your scansion. It makes you want
      To pick a bunch and say "well *that*'s a bunch
To be suspicious of." Platonic love is touch-
      Ing me the same place terror touches which
Is *no place*; suspending penetration so it's
      Intimate, but hovers, and I'm endless-
Ly beneath my apperception it's impending.
      Plus there's Aesop, who keeps gabbing about
Heights and flights of pigeons that just circle—*in per-*
      Petuum—our vessels. It's how we find a
Discourse for the void that makes our middle, and then
      Shape extrinsic threats around the pie-
Ty of centers. So I was psyching myself up to
      Be all, "launch yourself, like martyrs, birds, and
Missiles, little book; and boldly creep up in their
      Robes with words inducing hypomnesia."
But it met Socrates in prison, setting Aes-
      Op's fibs to verse, and so came back to claim
Some slippage in the politics of memory.

So I'm out in the agora lifting weights like
      A Platonic because hazing week's less
Burdensome for guys with hypertrophic forms—which
      One secures through metric repetition.
I mean this feather pen rips through my vellum. I
      Mean potsherds from that fabled vase of Aes-
Op's slip the clammy hands of balloters who cast
      Him from their middle: it's what he *gets* for
Gauging men by geeses. I conjectured there was
      Something lexic underneath that burqa
So I signed up for The Army—that's the liber-
      Ty to *lift* it—since an inch or two e-
Lucidates whole idioms of pigeons. A loop-
      Hole's just a syntax you can detonate
Your motives through; a man is just a grammar for
      Unpacking. It's like casting rocks upon
The backs of *pharmakoi* instead of looking in
      Our cups for stones and self-reflections. I'd
Meant to write this thesis for my MFA and
      Type it to a disputatious cadence,
'Til my drill instructor shot this mythic missile
      At my cock and now I'm ghostwriting this
Lovers' verse with phantom feet and brachycata-
      Lectics. So this account's the futile tact
You take in hell week when you just can't keep your shorts
      On. And I'm out in the agora shov-
Ing duck meat in my kisser 'cause I'm outside of
      My *own* work, thinking eating makes a middle.

Platonic love's a little bit like terror: de-
      Ferring penetration so that trespass
Feels it's permanently pending. In the meantime
      Aesop tells this tale of real impatient
Pigeons who get driven by their stupid thirst to
      Fly at painted vases, which we'd shaped as
Signifiers of our power. He was fondling
      Our earthenware while we and Greeks were clash-
Ing over wishbones from our sacrificial chick-
      Ens. It's how we knew we had ourselves a
Scapegoat. A loophole's a location from which I
      Can shoot a swaddled text refusing to
Participate in presence. I was fit to be
      All, "Go, little book; make haste to burning
Wigeons, and drop bravely in their cups like rocks that
      Make their waters rise and drown their faces."
But I had to write this envoi for my drill in-
      Structor first since I'd become the bottom
To his every ballad. Well you can bet that bend-
      Ing down to write is risky for a rook-
Ie. There's parity with reading there. There's silver
      Cups we sneaked in Aesop's purses. When he
Rushes from that precipice its potsherds slip our
      Dripping hands like accidental ballots
That elect successive pigeons. And Socrates
      Is versifying Aesop from deten-
Tion camps *despite* Aesopic ducks and Plato's mis-
      Trust of all poets. But a thirsty pig-
Eon doesn't wait; there's consonance and accidents.
      There's hazards under every damn djellaba.

So this account's the fiscal tact you take with whom
You have a touch with in precipitat-
Ing camos. I was sick of hearing speeches. I
Knew whom Socrates owed cocks to 'cause I
Measured all his cups as his accountant. Probab-
Ly I exercised this stick while I was
Figuring 'cause hazing week and hemlock inter-
Rupt your civic heartbeat. Probably I
Exercised this weight while thinking syncopes 'cause
I got real arrhythmic bidding little
Books to "Go; and forget about your littleness
And creep up like a loophole into robes
Of logocentric men, and unfurl like you've al-
Ways been a middle." It's tough to tell a
Cowbird not to keep his buzzing localized, es-
Pecially when telling it from poleis full
Of bovine. The birds are dropping potsherds into
Pitchers for the polling and it's making
Water break up in my gullet. So keep in mind
I penned this with my pants around my cank-
Les and a man in sagging slacks is just a syn-
Tax for undressing. Once Aesop had that
Little plunge the Delphians were pretty fraught with
Pestilence. I mean what's outside is al-
Ready in. And sometimes you perform the wrong expulsion.

I Was a Duck; My Shtick was Just to Sit *Here*

I was sitting and a duck and thus an easy target for words, in my sitting here I was privy to all that occurred *outside* of my cage through this hole in it, which was the cage where I sat quacking conspicuously like every sitting duck does. For lack of place in his cage my love stuck his leg through the hole of it and my bowels were moved for him my bowels meaning both my cock and my need to pass the corn I had just been gavaged with. You think this speech is real indecorous but given my engorgement on that corn did not exactly correspond to *my own* appetence and given I was only getting plump to subsidize the peptic labor of some epicure I can't be accused of pursuing that dish out of self-love or really at all actively. The hole through which my beloved put his leg for lack of place in it became a figuration of my emergency since it was through that hole I identified my desire which was no longer a desire for my beloved as such but for meat like the meat on the leg of him who was looking increasingly delicious, and also I realized that my cock and my bowels were the same thing. Naturally this made me a dirty duck. These movements which were symptoms of my own intimate hunger permitted me to identify that impediment between my love and I which was the screen of our adjoining cages in which we sat separately abiding in the placelessness of it. This was not so much a recognition of our separation as it was the crisis of my own confinement. By which I mean a consciousness of my own sitting duckness divested me of un–self interested love for my beloved.

Thanks to this hole in my cage I have some awareness of what lies outside of my cage namely a *bigger* cage which some call a cage and some call a city which is covered in men who are figures of men and some who are images of them. Prior to my priviness to images like this I would not have known what an act of terrorism would constitute but thanks to having viewed them I can now identify the unequivocal association between terrorism and anal penetration. Don't think 'cause I'm a duck that I don't comprehend your logic. From *this* side of the aperture I also witnessed figures of men like the men in these images being force-fed pork and alcohol, which happily *aren't* ducks, although lamentably they're wrongful in the doctrines of the figures at receiving ends of feeding tubes. These various acts of penetration I witnessed as a consequence of holes evoked some reminiscence of Thanksgivings in particular the one in which my father was stuffed with a chicken and then stuffed inside a turkey. While I have no religion I adamantly disapprove of the Turducken which is how even though I'm perched here just enduring in my birdness I can empathize with these men, whose existence is comprised entirely of penetrations.

Because my shtick which is my sitting duckness is prohibitive of motion I've resorted to *in*action as a praxis. Like don't think 'cause I'm a duck I have to ingest all your rhetoric. Plus the traumas of that holiday get pretty reassertive like this lumpen in my throat when I see stuffing. If swallowing is tolerance I'll ruminate instead and so become a vulgar poet with these remnants of dysphagia and refusal. But asking a text to speak to what I *don't* speak's pretty stressful—as if it's not enough to look like a duck quack like a duck be in a cage like a duck and because of being a duck on the whole to be generally fed through pipes. My adrenal cortex isn't mediating stresses real successfully because I'm *stressed* on this and cortisol secretion's wreaking havoc on my palatable parts. I'm on this hunger strike, it messes with your paté and presumptions about duckness. I might turn out a good lyric but I'm sure to make your dinner real inedible.

Templum

A chicken practicing his famishment still stomachs *some-*
Thing, which his stress is. A chicken getting grilled by chefs and

Questioners of chickens, stressing answers and rotisser-
Ie on fowl feet and skewers won't impress his Latin

Auditors: *they* lunch and stress in Latin. A chicken that's
For purchase begs the question of confession; but it al-

So stresses ties between the future and ingestion. So
You can bet there's been a shift in public emphasis on

Swallowing, and chickens. We're like, "well, birds have *spoken*"—like
You can't see the chicken beaks engorged with Latin letters

Thinking chickens would just *chat* like folks who ate them. I put
My hand up on this spit; I draw a space to pay atten-

Tion. It's shaped a bit like districts where you're plotting occu-
Pations. I make a line of lunchers on that pulse, from which

I pull out seeds, and meters, and tweet quotes, and make pulsa-
Tions. Then I triple grill this chicken so it feeds, and speaks,

And sanctions us, since taking auspices of birds that *hap-*
Pen to agree with you is classic. Man never grilled a

Chicken just because that man was *hungry*. In Rome the Rom-
Ans sacralized the birds who itched for lunch when it was *noon*,

And Romans lacked endorsement from the gods to get their clash on; they
Scattered crumbs like syllables and unchained all their chickens . . . but

Not before coercing birds to leave behind the letters
That would spell out: *Rome should go to war against all Roman*

Haters. Well, you might predict the misinterpretation
That's at stake when reading breakfast makes a hermeneutic

Practice. It's a pretty muddy missive when the chickens
Get political when dirt's all in their pulse—and plus it's

April. It's a pretty messy breakfast when men make a
Chick to sanction wars, then tables turn and soldiers break to

Eat the very *messengers* of gods at fast-food pace, at
Fast-food tables. It's a melancholy picture to gaze

Back ten thousand years to find we still fight wars with chickens—
Just with different chicks, and just with different nations. I put

My hand up on this stick; I trace an oven to ignite
That cool resemblance. Well it's out of the frying pan into

The fire when the chickens are in front of chicken kilns and
Kissing chickens. But it takes a little wit to be ob-

Livious to *signa* when you're seeking signs to write your
Own prescription. And if we want to keep on occupy-

Ing impulses of chickens then the chickens ought to *be*
Their cake *plus* eat it. So we thought we'd stage a small ingurgitation.

You Can Bet There's Been a Shift in Public Scrutiny of Chickens,

Though ornithologists make alibis for all the ones
Who occupy your Chick-fil-As and JPMorgan Chas-

Es. It's difficult to miss it when your governor "pre-
Dicts" just where the birds will land by filling earth with exes.

It's tough to wax prosodic when you've come to watch the chick-
Ens lunch: but they're in line just sending texts of pigeons kis-

Sing pigeons until suddenly there's all this vacant space
For birds-eye views, because the birds have flown—'cause none of them

Were *hungry*. It's a bummer when your dinner disagrees
With you post-dinner, but it's *shameful* when it squabbles pre-

Consumption: that's what Romans said when craning necks and cut-
Ting up the sky, so as the birds traversed *whatever* part

They wafted in hot air from gods, inspiring Rome to line
Up against passive halves and haters. It's how there's all these

Queues outside of fast-food joints and campgrounds. It's why augurs
Occupy their tents: to see which of the augurs pitches

Closest. So if the food fight seems misplaced, remember Rom-
Ans held that *nothing* need be out of place when *you* define

The ins- and outs-of-spaces. Like it's tough not to intu-
It that a Chick-fil-A will grill a *ton* of chickens when

Your checkbook's in the air like you've been spending. It's tricky
Not to bake one when you've studied bird migrations, and the .

Places chickens fall, and built an altar made of ovens
There. It's a pretty simple burden for the birds to be

Beholden, and to say, *behold, beholden birds,* 'til it-
· Erative discourse is the straw that breaks the chickens' backs,

Who crash into your take-out bags and help you make a case
For brokeback chickens. But you can bet there's been a shift in

How we gloss on immolation now that birds set fire
To themselves *before* you get your glaze on. Now the State holds

My binoculars before my face; I trust its focal
Range and all its recourses to lenses. Still it's tricky

Cooking chickens when there's pulse in your prosthetic eye and
Recipes demand you grill—*before* you grill, and then you

Grill *again*—each stuffed, thus inauspicious, chicken.

I WAS A DUDE, and paying for it with this pound of flesh I was indebted for. I mean I was tracking *down* that pound of flesh which extract would avenge us. But it's tough to track a pound of flesh when *every*one is fasting, plus they're nudging you with clumps of straws, all "*pick* one." The straw is like a feeding tube—except you get to *choose* it. It's why sand is in my eyes and why I'm agonizing about elongation. A penny on the water pays some interest when the river turns and Charon is no longer bribed with nickels. I grab this pound of flesh between my rocks like I grab *badly* every time we choose the sucker through sortition. I didn't need to *own* the cliffs I climbed to get my raid on. I didn't need to *own* the rope of which I spoke while sneaking into homes of men I've chosen straws for hanging. But the straw that breaks your camel's back might be the spitting image of the straw you pick to suck from *others'* pitchers.

IT'S NICE TO BE THE DIE and single out the blanks you're striking . . . I mean it's nice to be the guy who *smelts* so he can make a nickel. The straw is like a feeding tube—except it's extramural and you choose it as if *any* wall might be a wall for razing. Plus I was still a little tender from that minting that had measured me, and *kept* my cool as captains passed me planchets, saying "*hit* that." I grab gaps between my thighs where missing pounds is. I pack that absence on the camels' backs on top of all these straws I drew to see how many straws—and lacks—it takes to break a camel. It's like trying not to sweat when you're in Kabul facing llamas and your intramural mesh is made of llama wool . . . in *August.* So we took all their djellabas off and made them slip this ice on; it's the same ice that I've slipped on every morning since enlisting. It's why Greek cocks are puny on their funerary vases. The spitting image hits me like a metaphor hits Cicero: without a little warning, or permission.

Keep fucking that chicken.

Fox news anchor Ernie Anastos, to the weatherman

It Takes a Tough Man to Make a Tender Weather Forecast,

One who tends to the transactions between anti-
    Podes with hemispheric zealousness. It
Takes an interested duck to toughen up its
    Eider and contest the wind—*despite* the
Debit done on ruffled feathers. It takes a hem-
    Ipodal heart enfeebled by its *half-*
Ness to enact the syncope whereby tough men
    Contract duration when they count their chick-
Ens in advance of *eggs*, and hatching season. Yeah, it
    Helps to have some altitude to presage
Pending pressures—but don't think that that gives birds the
    Upper hand in storm predictions. My weath-
Erman helps manifest my restlessness by fuck-
    Ing ducks discursively and imping phan-
Tom 'pinions; it takes a phantom member like a
    Pending mosque to make a tender man tum-
Escent, since he correlates attacks on signi-
    Fiers of his nation-state with sexing
Sovereign subjects and their referents. *If you build it*
    They will come, and come, and come the forecast
Called, which bridged that discourse gap between devotion
    And sex practice, and semantically con-
Solidated clearing a prostration space with
    Dripping in our faces and disease dis-
Semination. It isn't just the coming that
    Repulses us; it's the real insatia-
Bility of entrance. So when the weatherman
    Was all *This mosque is gonna get erect-*
Ed I'm all *Fuck me once then shame on you; but fuck*
    Me twice? That's no figment in my pocket;
That's a growing pain.

There was this fervor gap; it marked the site of my
      Aggression plus the syncope where ten-
Der men omit discursive referents as they're whis-
      Pering about impending 'pinions. There
Was this forecast gap I narrowed by prosthetic-
      Izing suns with phantom blizzards. It's no
Coincidence our weather vanes are often topped
      By chickens: it takes a tender state to
Recapitulate—as *ornament*—the cock whose
      Coming clove our feet and fucked with all our
Meters. It takes a hemipodal man who's scan-
      Ning lacking verse to mark he's *also* mis-
Sing half a hoof, and draft a menu on an un-
      Hatched pigeon. *Passivity's the munchies*
For your self-annihilation's what my doctor
      Said about my akathisia. *Pas-*
Sivity is extimate and hecka patho-
      Logic's what the Greeks said from behind their
Grecian bottoms. You won't find cures for restless cocks
      Where Fox is wielding phantom mosques prosthet-
Ically to fuck a brood of chickens. So you see
      How it was crucial that I exercise
My fortitude by lifting televisions as
      The weatherman authenticates my sense
That there's a chill . . . and that it's coming.

A PENNY ON THE PUDDLE'S of some interest when the power shifts and you don't have a nickel to coax ferryman for oars to paddle back and pay your debts with sixteen ounces: so you *swagger* across riverbeds, on camels. The straw is just a tube . . . except you don't need lube to *use* it when you're swigging up the river to increase the distance between you and Grecians. The Greeks were lacking *lots* of ounces, limping 'round decanters with their obols in their mouths like they were mobilizing to *make ends* of all that lack, and limping . . . but better not to mention *lack* on lands of homeboys you might be outcasting. And better not say *limp* when you're attempting to make difference between you and Greeks, who take a bend to pay their debts on vessels. There's a shortest straw in every bunch: and then you make a sucker of its picker. But it's tough to track a pound of flesh with all this weight I'm dropping, and the straw that breaks my camel's back might be the straw my scapegoat draws when drawing straws to see who sleeps in freezers. It's where phallus faces fallacy, and straw men turn to scarecrows.

How I Learned to Stop Worrying and Love (that I'm) the Bomb

I was minding the temporal gap that extem-
        Pore penmanship makes when it *writes* pre-
Meditated missiles. Or I was messing with that chron-
        Ic gap the apostrophic figures when
My discourse doesn't *know* when it will drop upon
        Its addressee and bridge the breach that's per-
Sonhood . . . and prose, and math, and matter. I shift beads
        Up on this abacus; they clash like math
Is persons. I put the math in gaps so there's no
        Gaps there. I do this as propulsion from
The pause that's endless waiting; plus it lets me bridge
        The gap between the intimate and met-
A, printing histories of rifts upon the bomb
        Before it drops, and rifts unmake themselves
As they mark sites of making, and unmaking.

But imagine holding breath like you're a missile,
    Which just waits and waits until it's *ravaged*
By its own becoming. Like you could *keep* that breach
    Between the inside and the out, without
Your diaphragm contracting to a fraction. Plus
    It's tough to make a fraction on an ab-
Acus—especially when fractious beads address
    You indirectly when they pitch themselves
Against the frames of counters. Expressly when you're
    Pressing geese to answer questions math asks,
Like "What *counts*?" and nudging ducks you touch yourself, which
    Answers math . . . except you've cast *yourself* be-
Tween two pigeons on the wire. I pour some water
    On the abacus; it makes a gap be-
Tween myself and bubbles. I go deeper than the
    Navy does where water is what arbi-
Trates who's coming. Plus the *Times* divulged the likeli-
    Hood the geese are planning adding when you
See the birds on wires is pretty high. We didn't
    Stop to think, *that's just birds resting*. But im-
Agine fucking beads, or breeding numbers. Ima-
    Gine how I calculate by pushing bod-
Ies through the sand—like Greeks did—marking limits of
    Their functions. Imagine I can shift this
Itch from digits through deixis, so that "High jack
    This, fags" sexes weapons, *not* the I who drops them.

So I was witnessing the chronic gaps that extem-
  Pore writing makes—how discourse is a
Rift that forges persons—while transmitting wishes
  Onto bombs for *licit* wishing…which is
Just commissioned penetration. It's just like screw-
  Ing string or fucking distance. You can't pen-
Etrate a body 'til you make its matter *oth-*
  Er, or you ask the questions form asks, like
"What *matters?*" Plus my morning *Times* said "Pigeons are
  Arrears of us like Greeks on urns, with wing-
Spans wide as rips in all our breeches." We didn't
  Pause to think, *well, natch—it's geese, they flock in*
Gaggles; or that Greeks have made no *difference* after
  Centuries of making math on vases.
I shift beads across my e-book screen; they clash like
  Grammar's persons. I draw speech balloons on
Missiles so to bridge the crack that discourse makes and
  Fill the mathic gap that abstracts object
From objective. It looks a lot like mergence of
  This missile with my cock, but *that's* prosthet-
Ics of the sentence; there's no *touch* there.

DESPITE MY NONEXISTENT GAG REFLEX and flexible esophagus one time beneath the feeding pipe I was affected and vomited. There was a woman working at the farm where I was being fed she said you will forgive me my share in these proceedings duck after awhile. There are evils the woman said to escape which a woman would go down on her bended knees and force food upon a duck, but the Sabine women duck did not love the Roman youths any less that they were ravished by them. There are people all over the State who think well of me the woman said just go to the church and inquire of it. You will find I take the front row every Sunday and I pay my rent when rent is due. Go to the town hall the woman said you'll find a petition there filled with respectable signatures of respectable citizens the first of which is mine it demands action against men who come here filled with figures of men and filled with images of them and circulate past the holes of our cages causing us to sit there as do sitting ducks no offense duck and adulterate our morals. I go forth with good intentions duck the woman said and I've always lived within my income. You don't know how lucky you are to be fed this food despite okay the bleeding and your labored breathing and that makes you a pretty luckless duck. I know what it's like to be hungry duck but now I've got this job I've got my ducks in a row and there's no need to duck and cover anymore. You're looking pretty skinny duck the woman said. Now eat what you've regurgitated.

I acknowledged my sickness by partaking of it. I internalized not just what I bore but what I witnessed. I had a natural ability to gain large amounts of both weight and shame I re-digested my testimony which was the same as my vomit so *something* might hold it safely I made room in my body I was so accommodating. Even though I was a duck my breast was dripping with sweat in it. There was this illness in the folds of it which was my body which I knew from the duration of the pipe in it. My rheumatism started acting up in consequence of tubes and then my eyes began discharging mucus which the woman registered as sympathy for her former condition. Ours was thus a false truce over the translation of my speechlessness. The woman removed her glove with her hand in it from the back of my neck where she had been pushing my beak into my vomit. The preservation of my balance was incompatible with this and I fell further forward which appeared to enforce our consent over my consumption, whose corollary was silence.

It began to dawn on me that I must be a criminal because I was being treated like the figures of men who were made into images of them which then circulated past the hole of my cage. This recognition plus the woman's perpetual address to my open beak compelled my face to swell. It is quiet now the woman said from the edge of my bloated neck because it was. She said it is not flattering to my self-love duck but I sense that you'd rather not be here. I should owe you a heavy grudge for this the woman said but shake hands though I have caused you to suffer and though I have to cause you more. There is no recourse duck the woman said because we are at war and from its placelessness we're always thinking dinner so why not shake hands duck and be friends between feedings.

If a duck feeds only on himself then eventually his being is the same as starvation. I eat myself not to self-possess in it but in organic anticipation of *better*, which waiting only prolongs my despair. I don't desire any longer to consume my lover I don't desire to digest but *this* prosodic intelligence. I eat the message as I write it. There are origins in this, I demonstrate wholeness. I'm self-contained I don't need anybody.

The desire of the field is perfect: the length of its pull-
ing, the justness of its aftermath. Its fullness obvious
as the northeast if one is attentive. Here the many
earthly references to faithfulness: the grass thick with
variation, the cows in their dumb chewing, the deep
curve of their endurance. If the field aches it is only an
echo of its own enormity. If harsh, only the hardness
after giving wind permission. A feather falls; there is
no emergency in this. The cows think only of their
own thirst, the ease of its assuagement. There is no
urgency to grass. It simply offers itself, as present,
without oracle.

I Got my Grill on When the Chickens Started Feeding on my Twitter,

Though it's tough to pick the sinews from your teeth with all that
Gold there. I circled takeout lines from where that heat and stress

Were issuing, like modern augurs make the rounds of *form-*
Er augurs' camps to keep on grilling with their billy clubs

And *badge* on. Then I put up *other* other tents and kissed
On fellow pigeons. You say, "there used to be just one way

Of interpreting a breakfaster: and that's that he had
Spent the whole night *fasting. Now* a luncher's not a guy just

Stuffing chicken in his face: he's a text that marks a cop-
Ula between his lunch and all his destined dinners." But

Even *Romans* omened with the opposites of hunger
Strikes by making chickens speak like starving Romans. And ev-

En as I open kilns to take out chicks and bake out cakes
The heat is so inveterate I close them: as if prac-

Ticing enjambment on the doors of tents and ovens makes
Poiesis passing over birds, and birds who cleave like coup-

Lets. So we're like, "birds have *broken*"—like *you* can't see the fin-
Ished beaks engorged with run-on kitchen mitts the Romans used

To bake their own conclusions. It takes a little wit to
Miss the *signa* in your templum when precisely what you're

Waiting for is *signa*. It's tough to misintuit where
The birds will likely burn when you've been learning bird migra-

Tions plus you know what *kindles* birds: like when you circumscribe
Their airspace with the sacred. It's a burden for a bird

To be beholden; and to say, *behold, beholden birds,*
Who creep into our Twitter feeds, and always nest just where

Our lens is pointing. I pull out stakes from others' tents; I
Draw a space that I can shut my eyes in. And when birdshit

Hits the Twitter fans we censor birds from Tweeting, thinking
Chickens should just text like who *inspects* them. But the birds are

Still embodied, which means birds contain a limit—like the
Time it takes to de-beak birds at fast-food rates, in listless kitchens.

Tripudium solistimum

So we're looking for the word that means "the opposite of
Hunger strike," and thinking all that cake that drips from chickens'

Beaks will spell it. But you'll anticipate the misinter-
Pretation that's at stake when reading remnants gives your pol-

Itics its diction. It's like Publius gets grumpy when
His chickens won't eat cake and so he casts them over sides

Of boats to *sip*, since they're not hungry. It makes a ton of
Roman ships start sinking. Then Romans blame the chickens for

The burden of *beholding* birds, who don't just want to swim
In cake; they also want to *drink* it. It's a real distress-

Ing breakfast when you lay an egg that sanctions war . . . then sol-
Diers break to eat the eggs endorsing all their wars, and choke

On mistranslated shells that fell and fissured all their scram-
Bles. It takes a bit to miss a pulse when all of your in-

Junctions mean: *eat pulses*. So if the food fight feels it's out of
Touch, remember Romans held that if you draw the spaces,

You decide what's in- and out-of-touching. We stand beneath
The templum texting texts—except the birds, and tents, and tab-

Ernacles get up in our bandwidths: not to mention the
Decline of Rome was thanks to grazing chickens, plus the eth-

Ics in the histories of texting. It's a bummer when
Your logic stands you up when out to dinner; but it's worse

When it digests you in *your* kitchen. It's a little bit
Afflicting that we still contest through chickens, given chick-

Ens don't speak hate speech—or the speech of *what's-not-chicken.*

I WAS A SAILOR, THUS A STRAW MAN: that's to say that I was *set up* on this restless
and this bundled leg, in riverboats, that weren't my own to stand on. I was paying
'cause I couldn't keep these nickels in my mouth that I was minting to sustain
my own enlistment. I take a stick for shish kebabs; it turns out it's the very stick
inclined to prop me up in fields; I limp while I trace sites to make connections.
The semblance hits like metaphors, or Cicero in scarecrow drag: without a little
heads-up, or *consenting*. It's what we get for messing with the one whose straw's
the shortest. It's what we get for *picking* who will choose it. It's like trying not
to rub up on your private perspiration in Afghanistan, where ungulates wear
intramural mesh that's made of straws that broke the backs of all your camels. So
you see I wasn't queasy when they pulled straws from *my* person, saying "see how
much *of you* it takes to sweat a little camel."

What Happens Overseas Stays Overseas,

But what happens in the desert with our *hips*? It's
          So ri*di*culous it circulates like
Sentiment in Lady Gaga chatrooms. Perform-
          Ance titillates me 'til I come—with*out*
Extrinsic flesh to intercess us. Every ep-
          Ic enterprise elicits itera-
Tion, occurring first in poker face until we
          Take up tickling its nasals with our
Pom-poms and our remix. Still I'm pretty fucked
          By heritance, like Bonaparte's behind
Me with that sausage that he served to annex French-
          Men. I've read my Marx; it hangs on like my
Priapism. I put the *URL* in burlesque when
          Addressing all my peasants so the pub-
Lic's got a resource if it wants to check my potency:
          How quickly you cross *back* from drag is just
A mode of muscle testing. I don't mean to brag
          But I'm your videophone presence, re-
Distributing and multiplying sites of phan-
          Tom pleasure by perplexing all your lim-
Its of perception. Some chatterboxes think this
          Sounds a lot like **S&M**. A few kib-
Itzers thought they smelt a rat, but it was just a
          Pigeon. Or it was me, exuding val-
Ue from below my soldiers' threshold tax. Or it
          Was I who reeks of lumpen in this un-
Iform and manifests the trauma that you don't
          Know where my lumpen lies—or *what*, in fact,
That lump, and lie, are made of.

I'd been a duck; I'd been hazed and oversati-
      Ated. I had gone a little wild with
That manhood all behind me and then crawled into
      The desert to lay eggs in desert bas-
Ins. You've read your Marx; you thought my remix was a
      Clever farce, but Bonaparte's behind my
Camera, dictating my seity. Mimesis
      Is a model of applied kinesi-
Ology where muscles pass a pressure test through
      Preternatural flexing . . . on top of which
Okay, I have this dress on. I put the *phallus*
      Back in Cephalus as fashions haze me
Headfirst in their passing. I strap on hand-me-down
      Salamis because *that*'s reitera-
Tion. I come down to the cell block with my pants and
      Referents open and a camel making
Cash up on my lumpen—but I shake my hips hil-
      Ariously so the parody's con-
Spicuous. So don't miss in my dissension the
      Position that I take when minting sen-
Tences is: I become your intimate. Where they
      Breathe together, pigeons typically con-
Spire. I thrust my hips in loopholes where they're breathless.
      Then I post it on my Gaga blog, with
Poker face emoticons, in case you think I'm only playing.

I read my Marx . . . then went and vended kidnapped cam-
    Els, *internationally*, where you can
Legitly extract dromedaries' cashes. I
    Mean, the economics of my hips are
Such I shake them over borders when I have to
    Make like ungulates with fatty humps and
Thread the penal needle. Tradition weighs upon
    My cock like Bonaparte's old eiderdown;
This tickles me until I come—with nothing but
    His nightwear in between us. I don't mean
To brag but I'm that love note posted on your blog
    By Secretary Gates the day that you
Performed the *gayest* of your Gaga imita-
    Tions. As a missive I proliferate
Your pigeonholes of pleasure: and some geese will say
    That maxim scans a lot like S&M
Does, but it's *diction gaps* to capture birds who try
    To go sub-surface on my rhetoric. When
You're living in a loophole all that matters is
    You know which way the *top* is. I caulk the
Bottoms up with lumpen, then I put my little wig on.

It's a ball to be the camel passing through the eyes of needles with the very straw that broke your back, to *thread* them to embroider boats submerging under weights of men and semblance. The straw is like a fishing rod . . . except that "going fishing" means you suck up all the rivers 'til there's riverbeds—and pounds and pounds of fishes. It's not like apprehending flesh when *every*one is shedding pounds through fasting. But every troop has got a scapegoat with a little bit of difference. And out of the mouths of babes comes haze that pressures me to wear the skirt and put this nickel in my mouth like I'm your chosen sucker. I wouldn't need to *own* the bin all laden down with straws that we would draw from, and then measure accusations. I wouldn't need to own *up* to the pics I took when turning straws to figures. So you see I wasn't squeamish when they handed me the lightstick and said "light it up like soldiers *want* your photoluminescence." I take that stick; I prop them up; they brighten fields and scare the crows; they shine like targets, and like obsolescence.

It's remarkable to be the secret and to creep up on your keeper. It's uncanny to be ferrymen and board that man of straw that's both your secret sharer and your spitting image. But then I *was* that man of straw just perching on this stick, without a pound of flesh to make a burden. It's like Greeks with gimps hail Charon with their errant metrics tearing earth, and *ages* later fellow sailors waddle up to navies with an obol and *my* effigy to break the waves of rivers. We blame the sucker choking on the nickels in his straw because *we* swallowed something just as hard in hazing week when picking straws while wishing for the *terminus* of picking. And a penny in the river pays some interest when the ferryman won't take the one you give him, 'cause he doesn't trust a scapegoat who keeps losing at sortition. Not to mention that we've pumped the Styx down all the throats of enemies and emptied out the distance between us and Greeks: what separates us now is only scarecrows. But Cicero's not listening to how we forged *that* metaphor; he's thinking that the pigeon perching on the rope of Charon's boat is *nothing* if it's not my spitting image.

The dignity of the field is the sustainment of its humming. That there is nothing it does not contain or touch, that it leaves no remnants, makes no difference. If the trees wake in the night it is the sound of light in other places. Morning, memory unfurls, the cows curl into air, the air into branches. Each heals the others at their shared incision, keeps what the others offer, within. The day is always long enough; it doesn't break against the coming night; the two touch, dismembering their twoness. A feather falls at the long threshold as though falling were the only aim. It is sufficient, or it is not. And by this it is always sufficient.

Faking it leads to the genuine thing

Ovid, Amores

Cures for Love

" …And I'm immune to consequence, 'cause kissers' countenan-
    Ces get bedimmed because of taction." *That's* what my love was

Saying as he touched me. My camel chewed on cloven cud
    'Cause slamming doors had clove his diction. I had this heart a

Missile shattered. I notified the DoD so I
    Could swap it for a purple one. Plus there were congeries

Of birds just planted up there in the branches; and if I
    Had a heart that *wasn't* in my mouth but on my habit,

I could propel myself outside of that unknowing. I
    Pin medals right where ardent pigeons try to fly into

My breast; I don't issue from the barracks after dark. But
    Cupid said, "you *too* can make a steady heart arrhythmic;"

So I unsheathed iambs from the spathes of palms and psalms in
    Latin and, while Ovid's making deviled eggs with girls in

Ancient kitchens, put my paws up on his poems to detum-
    Esce distended couplets. I touch *first* to evade uncan-

Ny arrows. I always pack a lot more than a dozen.
    I discourse this to my friend, whose hands were never nailed

For love, whose face is quaffing ruthless waters under scrims
        And udders, and whose camels advance swiftly between sites

Of jurisdiction so my dromedary salivates
        With foaming gums to camel wrestle drowning friends and swell

The lungs of meddlers. Then Cupid scanned these poems I wrote
        To supplement my calisthenics—*plus* extreme gymnas-

Tics I coerced upon my friend. He crossed himself. Each mark
        He made was ictic. "Wars," he wails, "like diaper rash, are on

My ass, and *vexing* me." Well I wouldn't mock a camel
        On prosthetics; but I'd taunt a god with combat stress who'd

Been up in *my* muscle. I'd skinny dip in streams with crook-
        Ed birds so I could dunk them. There's no need to curl on wool-

En rugs beside your own extinction, to lie there 'til the
        Sparrows rouse the wretches to their work and wonder why you

Have a heart that's more syncopic than a birdcall. There is
        No *need* to live life as a pigeon, or a goose, or to

Be fucked by softer thoughts or else to document the times
        You've been reduced to humping bunkmates and/or camels. It's

Better to divert laments to flights of trifling birds and
        Not ask "did my love desist in tubes, when all that food was

Flowing?" Ovid said "exfiliate your neck from painful
        Fraises" during flour fights with chicks in primal kitchens.

Cupid, having overheard, withdrew himself to firing
      Walls and then undressed himself of sagging Pampers, saying

"Finish, then, what this Administration's planned upon
      My ass," and stood there with his splendid back toward me.

An Injured Pigeon Messes up Our Metrics When It Trips *in There,*

Interpellating us as ducks who *sit* like ducks
By creeping in our speech and laying stutters in our coup-

Lets. But catalectic couples are for *wanting*
With; and phantom limbs make ictuses that stress us out when

Scanning verse, or scanning our horizons for the
Origins of all our birds' afflictions. It's a phantom

Pain that hampers us from auto-implication.
It's a phantom adage ducks born out of double eggs spend

Ages after, fondling each other. I'm all
Like, *okay* lovers, if you want to love, you'll have to re-

Elect us. Our economic clock is ticking
Like a lagging metronome; this hinders us from picking

Up another couple dozen. Plus that Wiki
Leaked me surfacing from eiderdown and egging all your

Blankets. I hate to say *I told you so*, espec-
Ially since we're averse to *telling*. So we're sitting here

Like sitting ducks, since midterms dispossessed us of
Our standings. We're perched up in this semi-circle, sitting

On enacting bills—instead enacting all this quacking.

So you see how circumstance was such impulsive-
Ly we started *duck, duck, goose*-ing: you just lock the doors and

Close the ring and nominate a tapper. There's a
Goose in every gaggle, and my tongue's not in my cheek be-

Cause this maxim is sarcastic but to keep it
From that grain of salt with which I take "that soldier's not your

Honey." Other legislators want a hidden
Pigeon too—except they hate to sprint on eggshells circum-

Navigating ducks and when they're voting to up-
Hold the ban on candid geese, and *telling*. We suffer claud-

Ication 'cause we only legislate in poul-
Ter's measure. But don't tell a lover meter doesn't matter

When he's scanning lines to see how he's made lame be-
Cause of loving. I look to the reflecting pool where all

Those ducks are drowning. I'm all like, *okay* lovers;
If you want to fight our wars for us we'll let you. But first

We're gonna play this little party game.

Thicker lube means lesser friction. Thicker tubes make lunching effortless—
though swelling pipes to swell a goose's liver also swells your risks that goose'll
make a saucy dish at dinner. Bigger bottles make a broader neck to stash your
banknotes in and faster saturation of the sipper whom you're toasting to while
holding up your bottle to his kisser. I was hoping for a little detumescence. I was
accused of being a canard, or *telling* canards; it was operose to split hairs with
this onus down my throat because I'm lachrymose—and plus there's force, and
feathers. Semanticists will tell you polysemy's real disheartening when you share
a signifier with a common noun of questionable ethics. I mean canards are pretty
bummed about phonetics. Numismatists will tell you to reject a wooden nickel:
there's a copula you waste when saying *haters will be haters*; there's a shelf life on
a pigeon; it takes profit out of patience. It's kind of like a deadline on extracting
information. It's kind of like that timber that numismatists are hard on. It's a
little like this supplement they're pumping down my throat, except those cans are
efficacious *ages* after they expire.

Don't tell a legislator that declension does-
N't matter when the discourse that we *war* on wades—like wad-

Ing birds—in gender. Our jurisdictive clock is
Ticking and our scansion-marking cocks are just the ictus-

Es that make you want to duck my tap in passing.
Plus you're just a little vexed about the rhetoric of our

Party, since this game confines our speech domain to
Just two words, in passing—and indexically the heads of

Birds import the geese affixed to them I'm kind of
Urged to utter. So where's the agency, you ask, in all

This touching? And how do I seduce you when the
Only terms I've got are ducks and gooses? Well I hate to

Say *I told you so*, but we don't sanction asking.
It's a phantom pain that hinders us from self-incrimin-

Ation. It's a phantom adage *anyone* can
Make a duck pick up his skirts and just commence with running.

So when my fellow Congress-player is all: "*ev-
En I* can coast along the outskirts of the circle and

Get in just by discriminating which of them
The *goose* is" I gaze out at the reflecting pool, where all

Those ducks are feverish. As if there are no politics to *picking*.

It's confusing when your forebears use the crescent moon for centuries to govern their abstention, and then suddenly you're fasting out of month, and out of protest. It's disturbing when your Ramadan extends into Shawwal, and your camels get distended too—but not because they're pregnant. Appendices prolong your text so something's always pending, like a caveat enhancing all the currencies you spend to feed your pigeons. I mean for the first time I perceived my own appendix. It's kind of how a planchet feels when prized inside a pigeonhole; it's just like how a pigeon looks when pushed, like bills, in beakers. Don't think 'cause I'm a goose that I don't *get* your fiscal basics. Precocious pigeons always catch the fattest worms—until those worms wise up, and wake up *later*.

My temper's running hotter than those geese you're un-
Der covers with. I butter shifty biscuits. I'm just a

Little pissed about the general elections,
And now freshmen tell me passing laws with phantom limbs is

Simple? I retrospect my service days, percus-
Sing upon ducks until the Force, encumbered by their fuss,

Was all "they've adequately yakked," and camouflaged
Their quacks with heavy metal. You think I tell this anec-

Dote to backbite soft-shelled brothers; but how *other*
To address it when this honey in my mouth swells up to

Smother me? There's a goose at every table and
A fatter one in every dish at dinner. There's an egg

On every porcelain plate; I raise two of the ta-
Ble's legs and thereby raise the stakes; I add a measure to

The bill that wagers there's *no* legislator who
Can keep his egg from being curved, or having weight—*or rolling*.

I was hoping that the dizziness would lessen. I was sounding out my heartbeat thinking pipes are always pending, and then synchronizing sentences when *sync* went apocopic. Well don't think 'cause I'm a goose that I can't stress commensurately with my losses. I thought, I'm throating intervals between the gag and speeches; it's like the copula you miss when stressing *early birds precede us.* We thought a bottle stuffed with banknotes was an *awesome* fiscal stimulus—but didn't think that we would *be* those bills, and be those geeses. So when the Army put its birds in cans and promptly started digging and the price of every shovel swelled, we *still* missed its objective was: proliferate by laying birds, like *birds* do. Boy were *we* bamboozled gooses who'd been misinformed about the sites of value.

My tongue's not in my cheek 'cause I'm contemptuous
Of geeses; it's there because this grain of salt I take them

With has tasted on "that honey that's not hidden
In your bunker." Plus economies in which I speak are

Finite 'cause of party games. Other signifi-
Ers want a closet mister *too*; except they'll sashay o-

Ver eggshells when they're going to the voting booth
To uphold bans on wagging hips—and *asking*. If you don't

Know which the goose is in the circle you deserve
The right to pop the question. Here's one who refuses, then,

To swallow all his supper; his captain says it'll
Make of him the champion of fuckers, but *he doesn't*

Want to fuck: he wants to sit there in his clucking;
He's a chicken. That a goose can *tell* you he's the goose won't

Please him if the essence of the game is *still* to
Run down all the geeses. The virtue of the egg is that

It's structured like a crux is; that's why most of us
Lay geese eggs on our plates when we're in session.

It's befuddling when mothers use the crescent moon for *ages* to illuminate your fasting . . . and then suddenly your cranium is hooded and you can't distinguish gibbous moons from new ones in that dimness. It's puzzling to hunger out of month and out of protest, and disturbing when your Ramadan begins while in Sha'aban so that your camels get distended too—but *not* because they're patient. Appendices protract your neck so something's always pending: like the codicil advancing all the gifts that you're permitted to give pigeons. And when pigeons bite the bottle in the pigeonholes you put them in, you neither modify your system nor *obtain new birds* but shift the signifier of their hovels: *that*'s why that dovecote's now a columbarium. Semanticists will tell you this is pretty common practice, and homology is kind of tough on chickens.

There's a goose at every picnic making messes
Of your prosody, 'cause once you *tap* that goose? you've got to

Sprint a little faster. I summon all my Arm-
Y days when yakking ducks encumbered us with yakking 'til

We had enough to playback yells, and quackery,
And *really* heavy metal. "But come back to the party

Game and *fix* this," say the Senators; "we cannot
Make our eggs stand still." The trouble with the egg is that it's

Structured like an egg is. *Anyone* can trip on
The circumference of the circle and make fissures in it,

Intimating which of them the goose is—but it
Takes a Congressman to cause a stutter in the middle.

I seize the thing and strike its cusp up on the Sen-
Ate's table. I'm all like, *okay* lovers; if you want to

Carry guns, here's where my *gun* is. My tongue's not in
My cheek because I'm caustic but so I don't say *I told*

You so—especially since I just granted *you*
The right to tell it. It takes a phantom limb to crush a

Shell when you're in session. It takes a phantom fe-
Alty to make an egg stand still.

I was hoping for a different fiscal stimulus—or syncopes would tickle, or that coiners would stop humping trunks of corks and cork trees long enough for ex-onumists to stay hard on wooden ducks and nickels. My accuser said the word *canard*; I couldn't tell if he meant *speech acts* or meant *being*. But it's laborious to discrepate with obligations down your throat 'cause of phonology, and force, and lack of gag reflexes. When you're a duck, and in a pond, and all you *have* are liquid assets then it's central to your duckness that the flow rate on a bottle is a factor of its neck; I should know because I've got this one I'm throating.

Ducks born of dual elections sometimes linger there
To fuck each other. I've got this honey in my mouth; it

Makes a crack just like an egg tooth does. I set my
Scanning face. Don't tell a lover hatching doesn't matter

When he's hatching plans to make himself less lame be-
Cause of loving. Don't tell a vandal syntax is indif-

Ferent when he's pillaging your stanzas to find where
You draw the line at. Don't tell a Senator who's getting

Tactical in *Duck, Duck, Goose* a duck's a duck, no
Matter *how* much it looks like a goose does. Now if you don't

Know *what* that bird is, you can ask it. If you think
You'll tap the wrong goose you can just announce they *all* are. Here's

A gaggle that's dissenting, then, to swallow all
Its fodder; its captain swears it makes a man the ulti-

Mate of brawlers, but *they don't desire to brawl,* or
To be men—*because they're chickens.* That a goose can *own* that

He's the goose won't soothe him if the strategy is
Still to chase and egg down all the geeses. There *is* no bird

Who's craving to get chased because of gooseness. That's
Why we sit in circles to *choose* geese: so geese can't see us.

Expiration dates on cans are just formalities; they're kind of like vestigial structures. They're a little like appendices to military manuals: inconsequent until they're tapped to run for pressing functions. Don't think 'cause I'm a duck that I don't register your etiquette. There's a copula you pend when you're all *players will be players*, and your camels get tumescent too—but not because they're titillated. Canards and gulls are feeling pretty dismal 'cause of homonyms. Semanticists have granted that that echo is disheartening, particularly when you *sound* the sucker—or fallacious.

I look to the reflecting pool where all those ducks
Are suffocating. I look down at the egg, whose yolk is

Running viscous down the Hill, and seize a bit of
Shell to pool the liquid of my gist with. I'm all like, *o–*

Kay lovers; if you want to war like lovers war,
Then "love" our opposition. But since so many lovers

Love, this war is looking endless.

Now show us what you have painted behind it.

Zeuxis

Trompe l'oeil (nature morte)

A picture's worth a thousand prolix fictions in
        Your diegesis: especially when
You've been told to say it without *telling*, though you
        Might get outed anyhow . . . and *that*'s when
You insinuate the subject of your picture
        Is what's *absent*. I mean I call a goose
A goose; but that won't pay in cash the way a pic-
        Ture of a chicken will—despite it's just
A canvas that's *alleging* it's a chicken. Stu-
        Pid *birds*, who'll fly at *anything* that looks
Delicious. My earthenware's disturbing to your
        Camels and your misters 'cause it *seems* be-
Nign 'til rashly—like Taraxippus—it haunts your bud-
        Ding hunger. My thyrsus drips with honey 'til
Your hippodrome gets sticky. It's tough to run in
        Circles when you're just this *chroma* on a
Vase who travesties conceits of speed and progress.
        From governmental duffel bags I ex-
Tract eggs to mix a cup of tempera. Then I hold these
        Geese in place; and then I make a little picture.

With governmental duffel bags I creep into
        Your locker rooms and gather eggs to pitch
Them at your senses: 'cause a picture's just as prec-
        Ious as a dozen prolix yolks—like when
You call a cock a cock and cocks get pompous 'cause
        You keep on bringing *cocks* out. You don't de-
Clare a war before you've dusted sand from cameras
        And screwed filters on to picture without
Telling. Still, it's preposterous to win a race
        When you're just *plastic* on a lens that budg-
Es just to put the geese in focus. It's tough to
        Trust a fig when it deictifies some *oth-*
Er fig, which fig is keeping time with fags and sec-
        Rets. My thyrsis drips like honey does that
Glaucus' horses wish they took their master with when
        Seizing flesh like they were taking pictures.
But the essence of an image is it's *always*
        On the surface, like the detours of those
Thirsty birds who haven't met the mouths of pots and
        Now are getting pretty freaking sleepy.

Plato claims that painters misperceive their proper
      Subjects; he forgets that I've been glazing
Grapes and looking through these lenses since the *ancients*.
      There's a logic to the single sign; it
Keeps us all from longing. There's a logic to *Parr-*
      Hasius' logic, dumping buckets
On his sitters so that he could sketch legit as-
      Phyxiation. I'm all, "if Parrhasi-
Us had only had a camera: then his sitters
      Wouldn't have to suck on sodden cloths for
Hours while their painter calmly captured what their
      Truth was." But then I realize that dura-
Tion's what the *point* is. I set my shutter speed to
      Slackest. Stupid *ducks*, who'll agree to sit
For *anyone* ... as long as it means *sitting*.

The drift is you don't have to touch my pic and say
    "What *is* it?" 'cause we show it without *say-*
Ing here, while Glaucus gets devoured 'cause he misper-
    Ceives the appetence of horses. My brush-
Es drip with speciousness while hapless wigeons circ-
    Le on this bucket for so long they don't
Remember that they're anxious. But birds won't call a
    Grape a grape; they call it what a *Greek* calls
Grapes, which staggers signifiers like a potter
    Takes his potter's wheel and pimps his cups with
Alternating Persians. The birds don't get that some-
    Times figs are *not* self-referential . . . for
Instance when they're made of paint, and don't taste like a
    Fig does. I glance up at Parrhasius
Who's hung a stupid drape up on his painting. I'm
    All like, "*what*'s the object you're proposing
I desire?" I mean I got a little haughty with the
    Cocks of all my cocks out and the former
Birds—who now are spitting images of birds—just
    Getting frigid, making difference on my
Canvas. But then, I thought there was no blanket without
    Something keeping secrets underneath it.

It takes a lot to fool a goose . . . until you hang
    A *drape* up. It's rough to run in circles
When you're just this pigment on a cloth convinced that
    You're the one at whom you're pointing. I thought,
"If Bonaparte had cameras then his suckers would-
    N't have to sit and suffer 'til he crossed
The Alps to call their grapes '*just raisins.*'" But there's this
    Logic to the single place . . . and then you
Draw the *wait* of it for ages. I reach to drag
    The blanket back; my dactyls mimic geese
And crash—along with hopes of figs, in pain, who wept
    Beneath that blanket. I should have called a drape
A *drape* since drapes don't always mean that someone's *com-*
    Ing. I should have asked "What *is* it?" *not* "But
What's the other side?" 'cause that's what *birds* ask, looking
    Dumbly at my vessels. Now my earthen-
Ware disturbs *myself* 'cause I neglect its surface,
    Thinking what makes every vessel is its center.

My informer said the word *canard*; I couldn't tell if I was getting *laid* or *lying*. But it's strenuous to nitpick with this lightstick in my rectum; plus I'm lachrymose from laughing at our misinterpretation of *what's tender*. It's a little disconcerting when your fathers break their fasts with what they've hankered for for *ages*, except now their handkerchiefs are stuffing up their singing lungs—and plus there's narrative dyschezia, and chronic indigestion. We *knew* that when demand exceeds your current cache of fictions then your GDP is in a little pickle. But no one told us that that 'G' might stand for geeses. It's tough to stick a dead duck with a value. It's difficult to designate a waking bird as *early* when preemption is a problem, and contingent. I mean, a duck is in the circle at the right place at the right time . . . or he *isn't*.

In the fields form breaks, gives in to forces within it. What remains is enough: not mere endurance, but more, a fulfilling. The light a muscle, its careful arms. No accident of the body, moving or still, can make it offer less. The generosity of the fields is. If the cows have grief it holds them, makes a surface. We gather their air, their expanses, our names fall on them, our shadows, they stand under us, like welcome. The cows will be a quick humming, then vanished; there will be neither knowing nor sadness in this. But the field has dreams sometimes, where it moves things, and then they never stop moving.

Fine Feathers Make Fine Pigeons

Fine feathers dust on desecrated spaces and
Make spotless sheep *seem* worthy to be sacrificed

To sweepers, whose superficial fibers are the
High behind my cleaning benders. Poor *sheep*, when men

Of war use woolen mops to mop the rug they've rum-
Bled on, which was *whole fields* of sheep—which equals taut-

Ologic sweeping. Men trip on wool when shearing
Sheep to bare whole flocks as fleecers; and tailors can't

Align their twills and shepherds cannot burn their fields
When pulling wools upon the eyes and zeals of sheeps

In pastures. Not to mention all this water get-
Ting in the way of sailors. Poor *tailors*, who roast

Their geese on embers to put pressure on those sheep
And decrease creases. And sheep have filled the bucket

Up and sunk it in the wishing well 'cause they're fed
Up with drinking, which means we don't get our wish ful-

Filled . . . plus we can't prove there ever *was* a bucket.
I mean sheep have put their money where their mullah

Is so if we want to drown him *twice*, we have to
Go sub-surface. Fine feathers get my hackles up

So I can dust a pigeon just by turning all
My backs and forcing spines and scorn upon it. I

Know the sheep are sweating to resemble noncom-
Batants with those afghans on their laps like they've been

"Knitting." And shepherds burn their wettened sheep since sheep
Won't say where ropes are . . . but then, better not to men-

Tion *rope* in homes of sheep whose necks are wet, and pend-
Ing. Shepherds, toast your sheep—since you have ovens but

Not buckets—'cause they're wolves in woolen hoods in which
They tuck their lupine fur, and tides, and secrets. Then

They're taunting you by intimately getting in
Your faces when your glass is raised, and bleating *Can*

I bum a little bucket? Well boot camp didn't
Teach you how to inundate a sheep when every

Bucket equals subaquatic longing. But then
Sheep were always wary of how water sanctioned

Sailors. And sailors mop with woolen mops the decks
For *dispossessing* sheep—which just amounts to tauto-

Logic shearing. So sheepdogs rend the wools of sheep to
Help us decommission wells by sinking mops 'til

Waters rise and float their mullah where our gaping
Mouths are . . . but then better not to utter *rise* in

Homes we're getting hard in. We swept the fields for sheep
And found but *mangled* sheep, and crooks, and crooked staffs,

And passwords to the blogs of shepherds. It's a lit-
Tle bit uncanny when you're in the depths of wells

And all these sheep are looking down it bleating *bum-
Mer 'bout that wetness* . . . then you wake up in a woolen

Bed and realize you're just sweating. There's a passion
In the pastures; I'm like, *Greeks, go get your tailors*

To put pressure on fanatic sheep, and wrinkles.
I *know* a deep and adolescent envy of

The fucker; I know the hour for loving rarely
Coincides with lovers, and the gloves that tailors

Knit will keep the pimps who pump out wells from getting
Rope burn. But the sheep breeze in with afghans wrapped a-

Round their sopping necks as though they just got back from
Bucket games and swimming. There's a suicidal

Vacancy of rushing sheep who rush right into
Roadside wells to obviate their longing; there's a

Vacuum made by fasting lambs, who pump their fists and
Nickels into wishing wells whose dactyls help me

Rock my weekend cleaning. When shepherds pipe, then wipe
With wool, the throats of sheep perverse to fleece—which is

Whole *fields* of sheep—that's just like tautologic weep-
Ing. It gets lonely on this pastured peat; I pose

With herds; I hark for natural beats; at intervals
I holler "*rope!*" to recollect for bloggers how

Their moderator kicked the online bucket 'cause
Of shepherds. It gets *cold* up in this well of deep

Combatants' hunts for buckets; I emerge to pose
For Flickr on the milk-infected earth; the sheep

Are wet; their sheets are wet; their afghans lay upon
Their laps like they're affecting after-knitting napping. I

Know an adolescent rage of shepherds bleating in their
Cells who mimic noncombatants with their mul-

Lah in their mouths like they've been *gifting*. Shepherds, drown
Your sheep to teach them vengeance is a bucket. I

Throw mullahs into wells; they sink like nickels.

...be a good Pigeon to draw this vapour from the Head,
and from doing any deadly harme there.

John Donne, Devotions Upon Emergent Occasions

Cures For Love (II)

I sustained these losses and disfavors at the doors of
  Brigadiers and mistresses, whose latitude and fastness

Loosed the hinges of those doors so that they swung out on my
  Kisser. So I muscled out the dactyls with my esca-

Lating danders and unsheathed these iambs from the sheets of
  Hijacked Latin verse so I could predicate my mannish-

Ness on fat and phatic metrics. *Okay,* I bartered trag-
  Ic buskins for a single comic clog, since it's common-

Place to ambulate with one foot lamed when whining ele-
  Giacs. Now I've got the cropper and this pretty filthy sock—

Not to mention that I know where wits of kissers go when kis-
  Sers get to kissing. I abided all this biding at

Insufferable thresholds . . . and the only war wounds I
  Received were self-inflicted wounds of love, this cloven nose

From closing doors—and chronic PTSD. Your heart's moved
  By my stigma, but not broken. You're summoned to my ot-

Toman where I was warned that leisure leads to love, and so
  Went hunting to evade uncanny arrows. I ordered

Bridled bulls to bow beneath unwieldy collars and drank
  Bitter juices under stupid udders. I chafed inside

Of duck suits and then surfaced from that *no*where just like eid-
    Erdown and allergies, at cells, before my love had time

For blushing. I thought how Ovid changed his tune to be con-
    Tent with feeding figs to pretty girls in injured verse and

Epic kitchens. I don't project invectives at the lin-
    Tel of the DoD, or butter up its hinges or get plaud-

Itory, pampering its knocker. It's not the *door*'s fault
    That my love has used the door to bar love's entrance, or my

Heart clove with my nose, when lovers slammed it. I made my way,
    For love, through flocks of togas and djellabas, drowning hab-

Its—and the *men* in them—who mortified love's ethics, then
    Dismounted with these *feathers* swelling from it to extend

My heart . . . but the DoD deferred to swap a purple heart for
    One that got perverted. You wouldn't taunt a camel who's

On crutches with a cloven hoof, although you'd pick on one
    Who's sensitive because of strife and *entrance*. Time and turns

Of tune do sometimes sour tender grapes so Ovid sets his
    Teeth on edge like Latin damsels and their fathers. Did my

Love commence in boot camp, or the choppy flight, or headlights
    Where I witnessed birds in cross-examinations? Its foot

Was on my passive neck; I guzzled up the stuff of it
    In gulletfuls; I tippled 'til it trickled down my chin,

And 'til it tickled in my hinder parts, and hindered hin-
    Ges on the door—and hindered love, and further contestation.

SOME PROPONENTS OF PAIN AND SUFFERING and critics of animal manumission have been attacking my poems; the fact that my muse is a scandalous whore, or a little bit funny, or a terrorist has got them perplexed about my intentions. But then this Roman poet just said "suffer, for fluency comes by itself." The gavage farm folded after photos leaked the public had a painful time digesting. I was kind of like, *no kidding*. Twelve inches is a lot to put your beak around. I was shipped to farther cages; but they gifted me this diction, since outside my cage were boot camps where combatants did a *hella* lot of gabbing. Don't think 'cause I'm a duck that I don't pick up on your discourse. Soldiers mimicked on our syrinxes when sounding off in "duckworth chants" to calibrate camaraderie, and *counting*. They took their promenades in "goose step"—though they failed to waddle dexterously, looking less like geese than lewd robotics. The Army issued "rubber ducks" so fledglings could relieve their restless digits shooting pseudo-ducks and plastic, and "*ruptured* ducks" to soldiers who'd been honorably discharged. I learned that "laying eggs" is dropping bombs; a "bird farm" is a warship; "chickens of the sea" ballistic missile submarines. I discovered when they said *lame duck* it wasn't to interpellate, but gloss upon the metric loss in every elegiac verse, and *metaphoric* bird, like damaged aircraft. I was totally offended by these confiscated terms, how they defiled what my birdness was, perverting nomenclature into euphemism dressed in inept camouflage.

Twelve inches is a lot to cuddle with; it makes birds hyper-vigilant and keeps a duck from thinking of his feet at all serenely. You think because the photos ceased to circulate I'm eating what I want now. But a sitting duck who's sitting in the surplus that's himself isn't any *less* a delicacy 'cause his coordinates have changed and 'cause you're lacking the intelligence his liver's gotten iller. You don't reject a wooden nickel if you don't have cash for dinner. You don't renounce a damaged duck until his wound has turned external.

Don't think that my birdness precludes post-traumatic anxieties. I saw a sergeant herd some soldiers wracked by symptoms just like mine into a flock he called the "Brokeback Squad:" it's not just men who hijack crafts but boys who let their flashbacks come, and come again and fuck them, who repulse us. There's this meniscus in my pharynx; it makes parallactic errors and it amplifies the difference of our visions. There's a woman at the current farm I'm winking at so I can gauge our distance but this just increases weeping—plus it heightens the suspicion I'm coquettish. There's a lumpen in her throat; it's a consequence of swallowing while under obligation. Twelve inches is a lot to take your tonic with, especially when jugulars are punctured then you're swinging by your knitted hoof.

Silent enim leges inter arma.

Cicero, *pro Milone*

The field knows the difference between stasis and
stillness, submission and patience. Feathers drift over
it; they take each other softly. There are the cows, still,
their thick certainty, their intelligent dullness. The
actions of a body are not so many: it turns, it shrugs,
has will, has water. Breaks out each time it steps into
light, breaks in again, opens, offers, welcomes air. The
grace of the field is it is thoughtless of its own becom-
ing: what is beyond it, if anything, its ending. Its very
horizon renders that question senseless. Thus when
a field dies it does unwittingly. Its very attention to
itself, as fading, prolongs its dissolution.

THE BIRDS

The Birds

Prior to this tryst my debt was pretty damn van-
      Illa—*fictive*, even: I was inter-
Jecting *damns* into my verse to back up curses;
      I was bouncing up in fountains when in
Rome in simplex Latin. The foreplay was just pud-
      Dles but the birds got sunk in bird baths when
The tabloids bit the dust like desert geysers. But
      Even jokers put their pretty poker
Faces on when they're mistaken for wage labor-
      Ers who hang with birds until it's time to
Sell them. So I got into this motorboat with
      My capacity to purchase and a
Plan to *sink* transactions with belittlers who
      Requisition pigeons. *Okay* I thought
I'd do a little basic egging. I thought a
      Body without organs is divested
Of its viscera—so unfixed from its viscer-
      Al reactions—and thus free to cere-
Brate a bit and practice plural vandalisms. Nothing
      Bides within those membranes but my unfor-
Giving flows. Nothing saturates these lovebirds but
      A little tit for tat, and then the rip-
Ples over which I pass for overwater gifting.

. . . But don't ask me what the motive of this *gift* is.
        And even as I trespass to throw pot-
Latch down in living rooms, the chicks in opposi-
        Tion camps defer to feed like *chicks* do; and
Saint Francis is there tapping heads of fasting birds
        With togas, all "they used to be amen-
Able, but now they mock my *crackers*." Before this
        Stint my dues were pretty soft serve, without
Sprinkles; all that flavor was just flavored air and
        Sloppy distribution, and the foreplay
Was like licking middling cocks of middling Romans
        In the fountain drink departments of Rome's
Frozen open markets. Now the saint points up with
        Frosted tongue from ovens where he *clove* it
So that he can spawn a homily on dinner:
        But he senses *hella* birds are up there,
Travestying sermons. They're remixing ana-
        Tomies. They're making wars on innards. So
In this imminent apocalypse I thought I'd
        Do a little basic training. I thought
A pigeon without organs would be light enough
        To quiver over borders for irreg-
Ular rendition. I thought, those birds don't spin or
        Sew, but they get imped with pimping pigments;
Nor do they sow nor reap, yet take their cakes in cush-
        Y dishes: that's what the Saint is citing
About thuggeries of birds from where we squat in
        Stolen motorboats to make a backdoor ripple.

I'm in this simplex camouflage amassed for pet
    Shop scrimmages with lawyers. I've got my
Intra-gifting mesh on so it looks as though I've
    Simply come for *giving*. But the birds get
Pretty livid when you buy a bird for nothing
    But to prove you've got the *means* to make that
Purchase. I thought a body without branches is
    A bird shop without bargains: delivered
From division into lesser limbs and prices
    And so free to wholly register the
Pathos of the house paint that's my egging. There's noth-
    Ing more obnoxious than an organ when
You want to overflow yourself to waterlog
    Your other. There's little that's more fruitless
When the well is deep and we have nothing *in* our-
    Selves to *make* sweet . . . or to draw with. I'm all,
"I'm gonna need another couple dozen." But
    Then this pigeon gets aggressive on my
Soft skills as a sailor, and inscribes me like a
    Navy does—with cuts there. Saint Francis says
"I told you so; it's *mad* apocalyptic." He's
    On the phone to call in guards and navies.
Then he's preaching to the pigeons like they're *listening*.
    The pain of throwing eggs from boats is that
You're lacking balance. The problem without organs
    Is it makes a space for permeation.

I felt a body without foreign occupa-
       Tion's like a payphone without walls and with-
Out nickels: exempting one from auditing one's
       Purses or one's callers when the shells are
Cracking up because of personhood . . . and *static*.

. . . As if the yolks we throw *recur* to infiltrate
        The hoses that we lift to put infern-
Os out—plus geeses. It took a little Holly-
        Wood to ascertain that birds are pretty
Creepy. It took a little Murdoch to assure
        Us of the fervency of pigeons. There
Are certain flows and currents only embryos
        Can weather: like the goose-steps of their fath-
Ers or the thicknesses of windows that they're pitched
        At. I thought a body without organs
Is a nest without an attic: all bereft of
        Shades of difference between oneirism and
The *Real*, like symptoms of psychosis or a stor-
        Age space for forward-looking weapons. I
Induced ducks to swallow this in lumps in lieu of
        Chewing. But that body, it turns out, ex-
Ceeds its figure. I had a visceral react-
        Ion when the wrong side started swelling out.
I had this thing for getting *in*, dissolving ducks
        In wells; except when all the ducks were sunk
I was the last duck sitting, wishing there. Saint Fran-
        Cis is real bummed because the birds are hard
On sermons; I'm all *working class* to ward them off
        In attics with these feather dusters. But
Really I'm just striking at a solid lot of nothing.

THE BIRDS

Invasive Species

. . . so I'm up there with this kettle on my noggin,
Since amassing the ceramics binding birds by
Busting into *Birdland* with a wish to sip on
Duck soup in its kitchens (this notwithstanding lack
Of wings, while mocking poulter's measures). It's some sup-
Er primal power that drags nomads out of bed
To keep on comin' 'round the mountain when the cock
Crows. It's a preternatural force that fetches bath-
Men to their tubs and gives the cock a turn to take
A *dip* and cuckold all those washers. It's some sup-
Er shady mettle keeps this kettle on my think-
Er as I muse on Ovid's dim amend when Cup-
Id fucked his fledgling hexametric: to culti-
Vate foot fetishes and nibble shish kebab and
Grapes with girls in drapes, in antiquated kitchens.
But I've come to keep the birds from getting swindled;
To twist their little pinons 'till their prayer mats are
Unfurled, and so they're prostrating in airwaves, thwart-
Ing prayers, and peace, and textings. Like, how are you to
Think on *God*, or lunch, or rest, when birds have dropped so
Low they're tropospheric? And how do *I* intend to
Weep—for *Ovid*'s sake—if birds recall their kitchen-
Ware, 'cause pigeons *in*famously breed rotisserie
Disasters when their kettles have been bummed and
So they're krumping. I take this spit from kitchens of
The birds to skirmish birds with. But it's redundant lug-
Ging owls into Athens in my man purse when all
Bling derives—*initially*—from Athens. Not to men-
Tion Greeks read Aesop, and so *know* how birds were prim-
Al gods with untouched liturgies, and intact kettles.

I've got this prayer mat in my armpit so I'm look-
Ing kind of sketchy—not to mention I'm in *Bird-
Town* lacking crests, and nests . . . and plus all this *vexa-
Tion* when I want to get my *lay* on. But finches'
Foemen force the finch from fierceness to invention,
Just as Greece's haters impulsed Greeks to forge in-
Tensive fences. Plus it's only thanks to frenemies
That every Greek has Latin. I take the kettle
Off my head to better render unto birds the
Kettles that belong to swifts and wigeons, and my
Gaze falls on the favor as I pass it to their
Coverts—when I note that kettle's undergone some
Damage. But the thing about a bird is that the empt-
Y air *awaits* it, which amounts to: all that's *out
There*'s for the taking. I stuff my speech like it's Tur-
Duckens; then I'm all like, "*Okay*, neighbor." It's a
Wicked primal power makes the potter and the
Pimp pull back the coverlet when roosters get to
Crowing. Euelpides can vouch for this: more careful
Of his cock than of his eyes last night, and cocksure
It was dawn 'cause one was cawing, he up and left
His Aesop in the middle of the night and got
Himself a little whistle, and a *lot* of pre-dawn mugging.

Apotropaic

So here I am, in the
Parabasis, address-
Ing *you* expressly while
The birds bake bricks with which
They build their walls and break
Their kettles. I mean it's
Babylon backstage—ex-
Cept you won't find birds for
Purchase at its temples.
They've read their Aesop now;
Don't think those birds are keen
To loan out kettles. I'm
The chorus; *that*'s your fren-
Emy. You'll thank me at
The exode when you've learned
To hack an airwave, and
To cockblock gods with cocks
Out so your cocks brush dur-
Ing holy wars, upset-
Ting the hegemony
That's logics of erect-
Ion. And some Spartan has
Been castrating our ap-
Otropes so I'm on doub-
Le duty with my man
Hands on the members of
Our statues—*plus* my croon-
Ing. Let me tell you a-
Bout birds—the bodies all

Up in your airwaves prac-
Ticing prostrations aft-
Er rubbing up on all
Your neighbors' kettles. I've
Read my Aesop, too; I
Know how larks preceded
Earth, and lacking place, they
Made themselves a place: so
Every lark's a field for
Flow, and *overflow*—and
Hypercatalexis.
You men all made of clay
And shaped by amphithea-
Ter seats and shifting sha-
Dows, who once were *mad* for
Sparta and made vessels
Of yourselves to cache your
Fleece in when you lacked a
Greece to place it, who love
To skip your debts and make
A mess of expedi-
Tions that are hampered by
Dubiety of purpose:
I'm waxing histrion-
Ic thanks to hazing week
And fretful times: like states
Of duress, and undress,
And cameras on my frig-
Idness, and metric shifts,
And drama competitions.

The Advantages of Being Feathered

Like appetence, it tickles; the munchies I re-
Jected now all pending on my wattle when I
Bob my head for yessing in response to inqui-
Sitions. It tickles when that tunnel's in my gul-
Let and the corns are getting stupid in the pom-
Poms of my plumage, singing, "I'm a little ket-
Tle," 'cause they're imminently steamy. But the thing
About a bird is that it *takes up space*—and *more*
Space in prostration; and so *naturally* you think
I thwart your will to act, and action, and my mats
And nesting practices block access to your own:
As if access took a place; as if your God—*out-
Side* your head—takes a location. I'm all like, "O-
Kay, neighbor" when you bring back blemished kettles.
It's a ball to be just on the verge of buried
Next to potters when you recognize *all* pots are
Just a parody of gooses getting chased, and
Chasing *back*: and thus our potters know our truths like
No one else does. It puts a whole new spin on how
We apprehend reconquest; plus it's better to
Make pots than lay with potters.

You give your lovers birds as gifts . . . and then *reit-*
Erate that gifting 'til your lover's *sick* with gift-
Ed birds and cooks you both a *bender* of Turduck-
Ens. And the very lad who swore he'd never bend
For sex is bending over ovens—for which you
Have to thank the birds all fizzing in their juices
Which you can't attend the murmur of for fucking.
Of course it's hard to fizz with all those funnels in
Your throat. Of course it's hard to *tell it* when our
Money's where our mouths are, like Euelpides goes
Rolling on the real estates of Greece with mouth a-
Gape because he caught a glimpse of phantom pigeons—
And, on his back, unwittingly, he brunched on his
Own nickels. Well *that*'s a lesson in recumbence.
Plus it's tough to go to market when your cash is
In your belly and your kettle's all effete from
Over-rubbing. So we summoned men to live like
Birds: but now the birds inhibit your *attending*
To the play because they're in your line of sight, and
So you're missing both my hard-on, and the message.
Not to mention now the men are getting greedy.

Invasive Species (Redux)

So I'm out there at the clambake swapping chickens
Onto griddles when Prometheus rolls up up-
On his preternatural camel with his para-
Sol aloft to fend off UV rays and Zeus's
Apperception: like omniscience can be swindled
Just by busting out the baldaquin and shorten-
Ing your steps like you're in penance. But his fedora's
Pretty wicked and his camel's teeth are *blinging*;
So I thumbs-up the masquerade and tell Prome-
Theus he's looking skinny. Well the gods have got
The munchies since we colonized the ether and
Denied all further dibs to borrow kettles. Im-
Agine birds are in your airwaves just unfurling
Tons of prayer mats so your God can't get your texts—and
Now he's *wrathful*. Imagine putting fennel in
The nuker just as Hercules in buskins slips
In kitchens to salute you, and you're all like, *hi*,
But um, I'm making dinner. It's a lot like ket-
Tle logic when the gods pass through—pretending they're
Not passing through—so they can get permission to
Keep passing: but you can't *give back* a trespass or
The images you took when profiling pigeons.

You'd be misled to think us terrorists, just nest-
Ing in their frequencies as if there's no place *else*
To do devotions. But the thing about a bird
Is, categorically, it's *matter*; and it makes
And takes up space by definition. So I'm gril-
Ling like it's *history* this morning when I'd wet my-
Self with existential restlessness when thinking
I would share a fate with men in debt, and men on
Pots, and potters. Now I'm tickled in my beak by
Smells of all insurgent wigeons and I'm tickled
In my belly 'cause the more I grill, the *avid-*
Er your cool is. Euelpides can witness this; he
Once trudged home with empty sacks from being on his
Knees in fronts of geeses and he found me here, just
Getting *huge* with laughing. I'm all, *what's up Hercu-*
Les; I've got your munchies. I've got my headset on;
He's going on about invasive species; I'm not listening.

FENCE BOOKS

OTTOLINE PRIZE
Inter Arma   Lauren Shufran

MOTHERWELL & ALBERTA PRIZE
Negro League Baseball   Harmony Holiday
living must bury   Josie Sigler
Aim Straight at the Fountain and Press Vaporize   Elizabeth Marie Young
Unspoiled Air   Kaisa Ullsvik Miller
The Cow   Ariana Reines
Practice, Restraint   Laura Sims
A Magic Book   Sasha Steensen
Sky Girl   Rosemary Griggs
The Real Moon of Poetry and Other Poems   Tina Brown Celona
Zirconia   Chelsey Minnis

FENCE MODERN POETS SERIES
In the Laurels, Caught   Lee Ann Brown
Eyelid Lick   Donald Dunbar
Nick Demske   Nick Demske
Duties of an English Foreign Secretary   Macgregor Card
Star in the Eye   James Shea
Structure of the Embryonic Rat Brain   Christopher Janke
The Stupefying Flashbulbs   Daniel Brenner
Povel   Geraldine Kim
The Opening Question   Prageeta Sharma
Apprehend   Elizabeth Robinson
The Red Bird   Joyelle McSweeney

NATIONAL POETRY SERIES
Your Invitation to a Modest Breakfast   Hannah Gamble
A Map Predetermined and Chance   Laura Wetherington
The Network   Jena Osman
The Black Automaton   Douglas Kearney
Collapsible Poetics Theater   Rodrigo Toscano

ANTHOLOGIES & CRITICAL WORKS

Not for Mothers Only: Contemporary Poets on Child-Getting & Child-Rearing
Catherine Wagner & Rebecca Wolff, editors
A Best of Fence: *The First Nine Years*, Volumes 1 & 2
Rebecca Wolff and Fence Editors, editors

POETRY

A Book Beginning What and Ending Away	Clark Coolidge
88 Sonnets	Clark Coolidge
Mellow Actions	Brandon Downing
Percussion Grenade	Joyelle McSweeney
Coeur de Lion	Ariana Reines
June	Daniel Brenner
English Fragments A Brief History of the Soul	Martin Corless-Smith
The Sore Throat & Other Poems	Aaron Kunin
Dead Ahead	Ben Doller
My New Job	Catherine Wagner
Stranger	Laura Sims
The Method	Sasha Steensen
The Orphan & Its Relations	Elizabeth Robinson
Site Acquisition	Brian Young
Rogue Hemlocks	Carl Martin
19 Names for Our Band	Jibade-Khalil Huffman
Infamous Landscapes	Prageeta Sharma
Bad Bad	Chelsey Minnis
Snip Snip!	Tina Brown Celona
Yes, Master	Michael Earl Craig
Swallows	Martin Corless-Smith
Folding Ruler Star	Aaron Kunin
The Commandrine & Other Poems	Joyelle McSweeney
Macular Hole	Catherine Wagner
Nota	Martin Corless-Smith
Father of Noise	Anthony McCann
Can You Relax in My House	Michael Earl Craig
Miss America	Catherine Wagner

FICTION

Prayer and Parable: Stories	Paul Maliszewski
Flet: A Novel	Joyelle McSweeney
The Mandarin	Aaron Kunin